EVERYONE'S
Mandala
Coloring Book
Volume 3

By Monique Mandali

By the same author:
Everyone's Mandala Coloring Book (Volume 1)
Everyone's Mandala Coloring Book (Volume 2)
Peace Mandala Coloring Book

© 1997 by Monique Mandali

First printing, August 1997
Second printing, September 1998
Third printing, May 2000
Fourth printing, February 2003
Fifth printing, April 2006

All rights reserved, including the right to reproduce this book
or parts thereof, in any form, except for the inclusion
of brief quotations in a review.

ISBN: 1-56044-585-8

Printed in Canada

Published by MANDALI PUBLISHING,
P.O. Box 219, Helena, Montana 59624
(1-800-347-1223), in cooperation with SkyHouse Publishers,
an imprint of The Globe Pequot Press.

Design, typesetting, and other prepress work by
SkyHouse Publishers

Distributed by The Globe Pequot Press,
P.O. Box 480, Guilford, CT 06437-0480
or call 1-800-243-0495
Also distributed by
New Leaf, Devorss,
Koen, Baker & Taylor, Partners, and Ingram.

Visit our website and online catalog: www.mandali.com

Preface

A PERSONAL STORY

As you leaf through the mandalas in this book you may notice distinct Nepalese and Tibetan influences in some of them. This is no coincidence; each of my coloring books, and this volume in particular, is linked with the East. Few regions in the world are as rich in mandalas as the Indian subcontinent and the Himalayas, where they are as much part of everyday living as literacy is in the West. Two separate incidents led me to visit the Himalayas in the fall of 1996.

The first happened in Belgium at the age of fifteen when I read *The Third Eye*, a book by a Tibetan monk named Lobsang Rampa. For the first time I learned of *mandalas*, a Sanskrit word referring to both "center" *and* "circle". Instinctively I recognized them. Although my awareness of them never ceased, it stayed fairly dormant until 1977 when, having moved to the empty spaces of Montana, I felt the incredible urge to draw my own mandalas. I did, non-stop, for ten days. Afterwards, realizing how little known these centering, calming designs are in the West, I decided to share them through a coloring book. A second volume eventually followed. Before creating my third set of designs, however, I felt the need to infuse myself with fresh images.

The second significant event occurred on the winter solstice of 1993 when I was diagnosed with breast cancer. Even though subsequent surgery gave me an excellent prognosis, I knew that I had to reach for something beyond the realm of traditional Western medicine. To heal my psychic wound I needed to engage in a personal challenge that celebrated my health, my life.

One day I saw a photo of a radiant young woman on a mountain summit, holding up her arms in that universal victorious pose that says: "I made it!" Laura Evans too is a breast cancer survivor. In her book, *The Climb of My Life*, she chronicles her courageous journey from the edge of death to the victory of a lifetime. She describes how she and other breast cancer survivors made a heroic ascent of the highest mountain in South America, Mount Aconcagua. Her story inspired me. I too wanted to stand on top of a mountain.

And so, in search of mandalas and "my" mountain, I left for Kathmandu, Nepal. True to expectations, I found myself in mandala heaven: everywhere I looked, everywhere I went, I saw gorgeous mandalas. I absorbed their images like a thirsty sponge. I'll never forget my joy the day I showed my own designs to some village children and invited them to color them; they did so without hesitation. In fact, *mandala* was the only word we had in common.

With the assistance of Chitra, my Nepalese guide, I headed into the mountains. We hiked for a grueling two days before reaching a small village where we intended to spend a couple of nights. As it happened, our guest house was owned by a very unusual Tibetan monk, Kalsang Lama. In addition to his native Nepali and Tibetan, he spoke fluent French and English. He explained how years ago a

Western doctor had sponsored him to pursue a college degree in France. After working in Kathmandu for a few years he returned to his isolated village with the mission to give to his people what his friend had given him: an education.

For the past fifteen years Kalsang Lama has asked foreigners to sponsor local children so they can attend boarding school in Nepal's capital, the only way most of them can receive an education beyond basic literacy acquired in village schools. Like a proud father he showed me photos of "his" twenty-five girls and boys, many still attending school in that far-away city. Realizing how rich my own life has been as a result of educational opportunities, I decided to leave a gift I hadn't even known I'd brought: a ten-year commitment to send a nine year-old girl, Jyotsna, to school in Kathmandu, something she very much wanted but could never do on her own.

The next day, still wanting to climb a mountain, I asked Chitra to guide me to the top of a particular hill. A surprise awaited me at its 12,000-foot summit: an ancient Buddhist shrine. As I leaned against its white walls, surveying the quiet Himalayan panorama, I felt jubilant: I too had made it.

Later, as I was finishing drawing the designs in this book, I finally understood how these events are connected. When I was a teenager, a book by a Tibetan monk rekindled in me a deeply buried memory of something Himalayan cultures have always had in abundance: mandalas. Thirty-five years later I visited Nepal, leaving behind a gift that is similarly bountiful in the West: an education. That gift I placed into the hands of a Tibetan monk. And so it is that East and West continue to meet in my life.

A SPECIAL DEDICATION

There is a special design in this book: the angel mandala. I drew it for my young friend Christine Nicolai on the day she died. Feeling particularly helpless that day, I commemorated her life by drawing this mandala. I dedicate it to Christine and to anyone who loves angels.

WALKING THE LABYRINTH

The last mandala is a labyrinth. Unlike mazes which have many dead ends, labyrinths only have one path which always leads to the center.

This archetypal design has been found all over the world: in classical Rome and Greece, Western Europe, the Near East, Africa, New Zealand, North America, and Southeast Asia. The one in this book reflects the design on the floor of the famous thirteenth-century French cathedral, Notre Dame of Chartres, whose path pilgrims used to walk on their knees while reciting the rosary.

Today labyrinths are often seen as symbols of wholeness and transformation. They are built with rocks in parks or gardens, impressed on Hopi jewelry, and featured in books that describe centering experiences. When consciously entering a labyrinth in search of its center, we commit ourselves to a quest that holds many challenges, twists, and turns. A metaphor for life's experiences, walking the labyrinth on foot—or with colored pencils—reminds us that it is the journey itself that matters most.

Monique Mandali

Monique Mandali, M.A., is a transpersonal psychotherapist in Montana, and author of several popular mandala coloring books. She offers mandala workshops for teachers, health care professionals, therapists, and the public at large. Contact Monique at 800-347-1223 or via e-mail: monique@mandali.com.

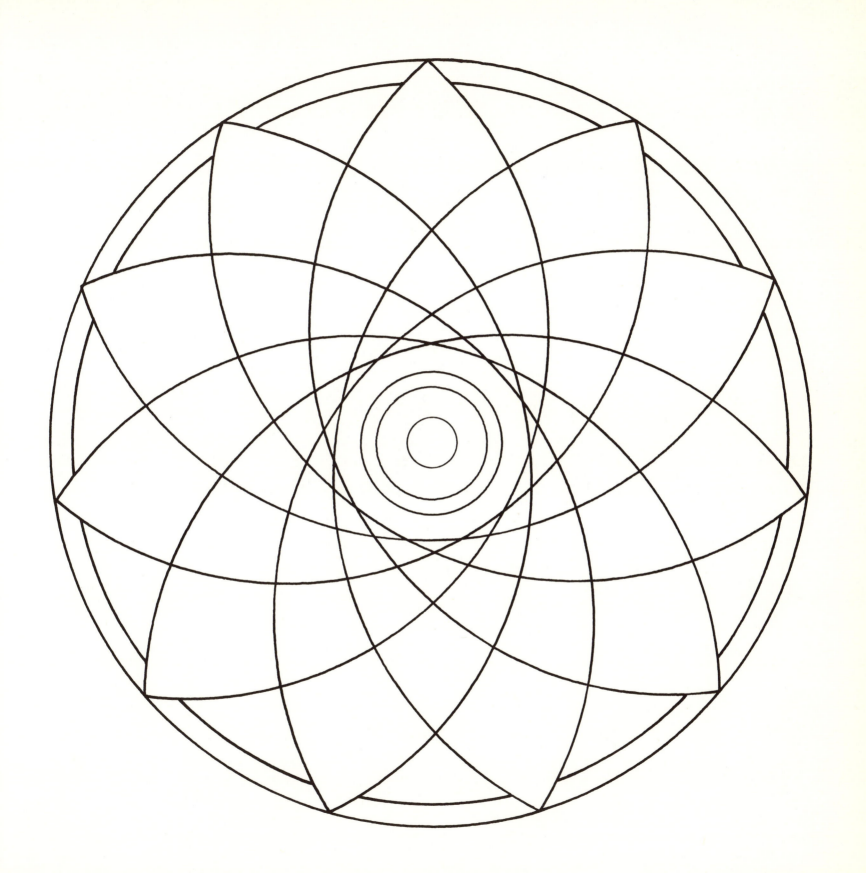